The Butterfly of the Cage

The Butterfly of the Cage

Prof. (Dr.) Arun Chandra Sahu

BLACK EAGLE BOOKS
DUBLIN, USA
BHUBANESWAR, INDIA

BLACK EAGLE BOOKS

USA address:
7464 Wisdom Lane
Dublin, OH 43016

India address:
E/312, Trident Galaxy, Kalinga Nagar,
Bhubaneswar-751003, Odisha, India

E-mail: info@blackeaglebooks.org
Website: www.blackeaglebooks.org

First International Edition Published by
BLACK EAGLE BOOKS, 2023

THE BUTTERFLY OF THE CAGE
(A collection of English poetry transcreated by the author himself from his original Odia poetry collection 'Panjurira Prajâpati')
by Prof. (Dr.) Arun Chandra Sahu
Email: sahuac52@gmail.com

Copyright © **Prof. (Dr.) Arun Chandra Sahu**

All rights reserved. No part of this publication may be reproduced, stored in a retrieval system, or transmitted, in any form or by any means, electronic, mechanical, photocopying, recording or otherwise without the prior permission of the publisher.

Cover & Interior Design: Ezy's Publication

ISBN- 978-1-64560-446-4 (Paperback)
Library of Congress Control Number: 2023945954

Printed in United States of America

DEDICATED TO

Padma Shri Dr. Jayanta Mahapatra
(22nd October, 1928- 27th August, 2023)

A bilingual poet of English and Odia, but internationally famous for his English poetry, the first Indian poet to win Central Sahitya Academi Award for his English poetry book *'Relationships'* (1981), recipient of the Jacob Galstein Memorial Award, Chicago (1975), SAARC Literary Award (2009), Tata Literature Lifetime Achievement Award (2018), Padma Shri (2009), first ever Indian English poet to become a Fellow of the SahityaAcademi (2019) and exceptionally, a Professor of Physics.

Arun Chandra Sahu

Prologue
(With an introduction to Poetry, English Poetry and Indian English Poetry)

"Poetry is when an emotion has found its thought and the thought has found words."

– Robert Frost

Literature is the mirror of the society, but poetry is the crown of literature. According to Jane Yolen, "Literature is a textually transmitted disease normally contracted in childhood." Dylan Thomas says, "A good poem is a contribution to reality. The world is never the same once a good poem has been added to it. A good poem helps to change the shape of the universe, helps to extend everyone's knowledge of himself and the world around him." Poetry is an echo, asking a shadow to dance. Painting is silent poetry and poetry is painting that speaks. According to John Keats, "Poetry should surprise by a fine excess and not by singularity - it should strike the reader as a wording of his own highest thoughts and appear almost a remembrance." However in the words of William Wordsworth, "Poetry is the spontaneous overflow of powerful feeling: it takes its origin from emotion recollected in tranquility." T.S. Eliot opines "Genuine poetry can communicate before it is understood." The former President of India, A.P.J. Abdul

Kalam comments, "Poetry comes from the highest happiness or the deepest sorrow."

Poetry is the music of words and language of heart. It arouses peace and tranquility in the soul and mind; unconsciously ameliorates passion towards life, praising the beauties of nature, loving all elements of the universe and understanding philosophy of life and death, myth and mystery.

All the ornaments of poetry: rhyme and rhythm, simile and metaphor, allegory and alliteration, apostrophe and imagery are sparkling continuously and constantly from the past to present. Poetry has varied positive effects on human civilization from time immemorial. A good poem may leave an indelible impression in the heart of a person. First, poetry had originated in past probably 5000 years ago and then came the prose in later period in the late ninth century. All the mythological documents were in poetry. In ancient times people could memorize and recite hymns of *Vedas* (1500-1000 B.C.), which were in the form of poetry in Sanskrit and continued for generations for which *Veda* is otherwise known as '*Shruti*'. The famous Indian Sanskrit epics *Ramayana* and *Mahabharata* are some of the oldest epic poetry. *Mahabharata* according to some scholars, is the longest epic poetry of the world. Poetry appears among the earliest records of most literate cultures, with poetic fragments found on early monoliths, rune stones and stelae. The Deluge tablet, carved in stone, of the Epic of *Gilgamesh* in Akkadian written in cuneiform dates back to second millennium B.C.

Poetry is an oral art form which predates written text. The earliest poetry is believed to have been recited or sung, employed as a way of remembering oral history, genealogy and law. Poetry is often closely related to musical traditions.

The earliest poetry exists in the form of hymns, such as the poetry of Sumerian priestess Enheduanna and other types of songs such as chants. Thus poetry is a verbal art. A rhythmic and repetition form would make a long story easier to remember and retell, before writing was available as a reminder. Also *Odyssey* (800-675 B.C.) appears to have been composed in poetic form to aid memorization and oral transmission in prehistoric and ancient societies.

In Africa, poetry has a history dating back to prehistoric times with the creation of hunting poetry, panegyric and elegiac court poetry. Some of the earliest written poetry in Africa can be found among the Pyramid Texts written during the 25th century B.C., while the epic of *Sundiate* is one of the most well-known examples of griot court poetry.

The oldest surviving speculative fiction poem from Ancient Egypt is the *'Tale of the Shipwrecked Sailor'*, written in Hieratic dates back to around 2500 B.C.E. The other oldest epic poetry are the Greek mythological epic, *'Iliad'* and *'Odyssey'* both by Homer (translation of *Odyssey* by T.E. Shaw published by Oxford University Press in 1951), *Tibetan Epic of King Gesar* apart of Indian epic *'Ramayana'* and *'Mahabharata'*. Some scholars believe that either the *Mahabharata* or the *Tibetan Epic of King Gesar* is the longest epic poetry in history.

Ancient thinkers sought to determine what makes poetry distinctive as a form and what distinguishes good poetry from bad, resulting in the development of *'poetics'* or the study of the aesthetics of poetry. Context can be critical to poetics and to the development of poetic genres and forms, e.g. poetry employed to record historical events in epics such as *Gilgamesh* or Ferdowsi's *Shahnameh*. But poetry used for liturgical purposes in hymns, psalms, suras and hadiths has an inspirational tone, whereas, elegies and tragedy are intended to evoke deep internal emotional responses.

Classical thinkers classified poetry as a way to define and assess the quality of poetry, e.g. Aristotle's poetics narrates the three genres of poetry : the epic, comic and tragic and develops rules to distinguish the highest quality poetry of each genre. Later aestheticians identified three major genres : epic poetry, lyric poetry and dramatic poetry (includes comedy and tragedy).

The Classic of Poetry, often known by its original name of the *Odes* or *Poetry* is the earliest existing collection of 305 Chinese poems and songs dating from the 11th to the 7th century B.C. The stylistic development of classical Chinese poetry consists of both literary and oral cultural processes. The poems preserved in written form constitute the poetic literature.

Sonnet form of poetry appeared in the 13th century. While many of us simply learned to distinguish between Petrarchan (Italian) and Shakespearean sonnets in a high school or college English classes, it's important to know that these works are fundamental to the history of verse. Traditionally, sonnets are written in iambic pentameter and the rhyme scheme varies in Italian and English poems. Francesco Petrarca of Italy for whom the Petrarchan sonnet is named, is perhaps one of the most famous early writers of sonnet in 14th century. It became best known as an English poetic form through the works of William Shakespeare in the 16th century. Sonnet 18 is the most famous poem of Shakespeare and among the most renowned sonnets ever written entitled "Shall I compare thee to a summer's day". He has published 154 sonnets in his 'Quarto' in 1609 which he wrote throughout his career.

The themes of these sonnets are: the passage of time, mortality, love, beauty, infidelity and jealously etc. The first 126 sonnets are addressed to a young man and the last 28 addressed to a woman – a mysterious 'dark lady'. Elizabethan poetry of the 1500s shifted into Restoration poetry and a marked turn away from the sonnet. The Restoration poetry of the 17th century includes satirical verses of John Dryden and Alexander Pope.

John Milton's *'Paradise Lost'* (1667), a story of fallen pride, was the first major poem to appear in England after the Restoration, during the period of religious and political instability. He is the last major poet of the English Renaissance. His later major works include *'Paradise Regained'* (1671) and *'Samson Agonistes'* (1671). Milton's works reflect deep personal convictions, a passion for freedom and self-determination.

In 18th century, the romantic movement in English poetry emerged. The famous poets of this movement were William Blake, William Wordsworth, Samuel Taylor Coleridge, Percy Bysshe Shelley, Lord Byron and John Keats etc. The Lyrical Ballads of Wordsworth and Coleridge (1798) were worthy to be noted. Shelley is the most famous for classic anthology verse works as *'Ozymardias'* and his ground breaking poem *'The Masque of Anarchy'* calls for nonviolence in protest and political action. Mahatma Gandhi's passive resistance was influenced and inspired by Shelley's verse. In Shelley's "Defense of Poetry" he contends that poets are the "creators of language" and that the poet's job is to refresh language of their society.

The Victorian era in the 19th century was a period of great political, social and economic change. The major Victorian poets were John Clare, Alfred, Lord Tennyson, Robert Browning, Elizabeth Barrett Browning, Matthew

Arnold, Christiana Rossetti, Dante Gabriel Rossetti, R.L. Stevenson, Oscar Wilde, W.B. Yeats, Rudyard Kipling, Thomas Hardy and G.M. Hopkins. John Clare came to be known for his celebratory representation of the English countryside and his lamentation of its disruption. No one has ever written more powerfully of nature, of a rural childhood and of the alienated and unstable self. Hopkins wrote in relative obscurity with unusual style (sprung rhythm and heavy reliance on rhyme and alliteration). Also comic verse abounded in the Victorian era like Bab Ballads.

The Victorian era continued into the early 20th century. W.B. Yeats and Thomas Hardy emerged as the leading representatives of the poetry of the old era to act as a bridge into the new. The Georgian poets were the first major grouping by the post-Victorian era. They were Edmund Blunden, Rupert Brooke, Robert Graves, D.H. Lawrence, Water de la Mare and Siegfried Sassoon. Their poetry represented something of a reaction to the decadence and tended towards the sentimentality. Brook and Sassoon won reputations as war poets and Lawrence was associated with the modernist movement. The other notable poets who wrote about the war include Issac Rosenberg, Edward Thomas, Wilfred Owen, May Cannan, Thomas Hardy and Rudyard Kipling.

The modern English poets in early twentieth century are T.S. Eliot, Gertrude Stein, Ezra Pound, David Jones etc. Eliot, particularly after the publication of 'The Waste Land', became a major figure and influenced other English poets.

The famous Indian poet Rabindranath Tagore (1861-1941) was awarded the Nobel prize in literature in 1913 for his best-known poetry collection *'Gitanjali'* (Song Offerings) being translated by him from his original Bengali poetry collection *'Gitanjali'*, with an introduction by W.B. Yeats published by MacMillan and Co. Ltd. London, also in 1913. Tagore's poetic style can be perceived from the following lines from Gitanjali :

> 'My eyes strayed far and wide before I shut them and said 'Here art thou !'
> The question and the cry 'Oh, where ?'
> Melt into tears of a thousand streams and deluge the world with the flood of the assurance 'I am !'
> – Song XII, Gitanjali, 1913.

Tagore was influenced by the atavistic mysticism of Vyasa and other rishi-authors of the *Upanishads*, the Bhakti-Sufi mystic Kabir and Ramprasad Sen. His most innovative and mature poetry embodies his exposure to Bengali rural folk music, which included mystic Baul Ballads.

The development of modern poetry is generally seen as having started of the beginning of 20th century and extends into the 21st century. Among its major American poets who write in English are T. S. Eliot, Robert Frost, Wallace Stevens, Maya Angelou, June Jerdan, Allen Ginsberg, Nobel laureate Louise Glück and Sylvia Plath. Among the modern epic poets are Ezra Pound, Derek Walcott (Nobel laureate for Literature in 1992) and Giannina Braschi. Contemporary poets Joy Harjo, Kevin Young and Natasha Trethewey compose poetry in the lyric form. The use of verse to transmit cultural information is *in vogue* today. Poets are now writing more for the eye than for the ear.

The development of literacy gave rise to more personal, shorter poems intended to be sung are called lyrics (Greek *lura* or *lyre* meaning a stringed musical instrument). In more recent times, the introduction of electronic media and the rise of the poetry reading have led to resurgence of performance poetry in the lyric genre, including open mic lyric monologues and poetry slam competitions.

Geoffrey Hill is considered as the finest English poet of recent years. There has also been a growth in interest in women's writing and in poetry from England's minorities, especially the West Indian Community. Some famous poets who emerged in recent period include Carol Ann Duffy, Andrew Motion, Craig Raine, Wendy Cope, James Fenton, Blake Morrison, L. K. Johnson, Benjamin Zephaniah, Glyn Maxwell, Selima Hill, Michel Hofmann, Dan Paterson, Julia Copus, Alice Oswald, Tony Lopez, and Allen Fisher.

Indian poetry has a long and rich history dating back to ancient times. Due to the diverse nature of India, Indian poetry has been written in numerous languages including Sanskrit, Hindi, Odia, Tamil, Telugu, Kannada, Bengali and Urdu as well as in foreign languages like English and Persian. The most significant feature of Indian literature is its diversity which is due to the country's variety of languages and sub-cultures. Indian poetry is one of the greatest genres. Indian poets have been writing in English since the early 19th century and their poems are widely read all the world over. Some famous Indian English poets those who stood out over time for their unique influences on modern Indian English poetry include Jayanta Mahapatra, Sarojini Naidu, Nissim Ezekiel, Sri Aurobindo Ghosh, Kamala Das, (Kamala Surayya), A. K. Ramanujan, apart from Nobel laureate Rabindranath Tagore.

Jayanta Mahapatra (1928) of Odisha, a retired professor of physics, is an outstanding Indian English poet of post-independent India, to whom I have dedicated this poetry collection of mine, as I am also born and brought up in Odisha, retired as a professor of botany and has keen interest in literature including poetry (both Odia and English), short story and popular science. His poems explore intricate human relationships. A major source for his poetry's vivid imagery is the landscape of Odisha and surroundings. Mahapatra's acute and ironic observations of life make his poetry appeal to all types of readers. He has authored 27 books of poems out of which seven are in Odia and the rest in English. His poetry collections include Relationship, Bare Face, Shadow Space, A Father's Hours, A Rain of Rites, The False Start, Close the Sky Ten by Ten, Waiting etc. He writes in free verse, uses the colloquial tone and wants to explore the uncertainties and the intricacies of life. He has adopted certain techniques to explore such themes as love, death, exploitations of women and projected the images of women in his poetry which are unique as they exist without emotion and identity. His poems 'Indian Summer' and 'Hunger' are regarded as classics in modern Indian English literature.

'Long and lean, her years were cold as rubber.
She opened her wormy legs wide.
I felt the hunger there,
the other one, the fish slithering
turning inside.'

– 'Hunger'
Jayanta Mahapatra

Mahapatra is a part of a trio of poets who laid the foundations of Indian English poetry, which includes A. K. Ramanujan (from Karnatak), R. Parthasarathy apart from him. He differed from others in not being a product of Bombay school of poets. Over time, he has managed to carve a quiet, tranquil poetic voice of his own, different from those of his contemporaries. Mahapatra's poems have appeared in prestigious poetry anthologies like 'The Dance of the Peacock' : An Anthology of English Poetry from India, published by Hidden Brook Press, Canada.

Sarojini Naidu (1879-1949) known as the 'Nightingale of India', was one of India's most famous female poets. The major themes of her poems are search for pure love, seeking comfort in natural beauty and everyday experiences of life.

Sri Aurobindo Ghosh is one of the few Indian poets who could blend both western and eastern poetic sensibilities. His poems, which touch on metaphysical themes, express his ardent philosophy of life and mystic thoughts. His most famous works are 'The Life Divine' and 'Savitri'.

Kamala Das (1934–2009) is the most famous female English-language poet in India. Her poems appear in the syllabi of literary studies of many international universities. Her work is the ardent expression of a very sensitive soul always on the search of pure and intense love without restrictions. A. K. Mehrotra's poems are ironical depictions of modern reality with a touch of surrealism. Gieve Patel depicts contemporary reality with pungent humour and a crude sense of irony. Daruwalla's poems speak of deep concerns for nature and expose man's cruelty to it. A. K. Ramanujan is considered as a 'perfect poet' as he uses language, images, irony and varied themes effortlessly.

Although many think back to the poets of the Romantic or Modern movements when they consider great poetic works, the writers of today have as much, if not more, to say about the frustrating and beautiful complexities of human experience. Some wonderful poets of the 21st century who have contributed some incredible verse in the last two decades are Seamus Heaney of Ireland (Nobel laureate of 1995 for literature), Fleur Adcock of New Zealand, Wendell Berry, J. C. Oates of New York, Margaret Atwood of Canada, Vikram Seth of Kolkata, Sherman Alexie of Washington, Carol Ann Duffy of Scotland, Billy Collins of America, Derek Walcott of Saint Lucia, an Island country in the West Indies and Simon Robert Armitage of England.

While modern poetry or the poetry evolving in the twenty first century has adopted a more favourable style towards free verse and a greater emphasis on artistic expression, it has evolved with features like blank verse, disrupted or unkempt syntax, irregular stanza structure and lacking rhyme schemes. The 21st century digital poetry is the metamorphosis of an archaic art form. New popularity for poetry has been achieved through big portals on social media platforms, giving new artists and writers a space to showcase their works. Social media, one of the biggest boons for a lot of business in the 21st century has also been a big platform for many poets and writers as well as other artists to showcase their works and achieve fame. Poetry has evolved to become a highly appreciative art form.

Online or Instagram poetry has become the biggest source of artistic influence on social media. It started back in 2012, when the poet Lang Leav started publishing her works online on instagram having around half a million instagram followers. Canadian poet Atticus (anonymous) is also an instagram celebrity poet publishing online since 2013. Instagram poetry was once again revolutionized by the Indian origin Canada based poet Rupi Kaur who became a big success with two publications and two world tours. Her poetry focuses on the diaspora, the brown values and love loss among other things. In the world of today, her bold, honest and powerful messages are as important as ever. Few lines of her poem :

> 'When death
> takes my hand
> i will hold you with the other
> and promise to find you
> in every lifetime.'
>   – Commitment.

Other prominent names include Pierre A. Jeanty, Nayyirah Waheed etc.

Coming to my present anthology of 51 poems, 'The Butterfly of the Cage' is the English transcreation of my original collection of Odia poems entitled 'Panjurira Prajâpati' (2017). Most of its Odia poems have been published in various Odia magazines and a few of its English version has also been published in some magazines during 2014-22. This work is my ninth poetry collection and the second transcreation to English after my first transcreation 'The Rainbow in Darkness' from my original Odia poetry anthology 'Andhârare Indradhanu'. The title of the present anthology is after its first poem 'The Butterfly of the Cage' which reminds the metamorphosis of the hero of the novella 'The Metamorphosis' by Franz Kafka (1915), to a strange huge insect one morning and how he struggles to adjust to this new condition. This poem of mine depicts how a caterpillar in an iron cage has metamorphosed to a butterfly and subsequently to winged termites, then to ants and flies, subsequently to bacteria and viruses and ultimately to invisible God particles which are subatomic particles of our universe and the 2013 Nobel prize in Physics was awarded for its discovery. Thus this poem ends with an element of scientific conception which rarely finds its place in poetry. However in the present twenty first century, general people are well acquainted with the common scientific development, discoveries and inventions for example the smart mobile phones, television, laptops, 3-D cinemas, spacecraft etc.

The second poem of this anthology 'Travelling Aboard' illustrates some important tourist destinations of a number of countries outside India and the loveliness of our earth and ends with the philosophy of life, culminating in death.

The third poem 'Conversation with God' is a satirical poem with the accusation of a wife to God for her childlessness. The fourth poem is a realization of the existence of God and some other poems are also versed about God. The poems of this anthology are not based on a particularly theme but on varied themes like human desire and despair, helplessness and loneliness, agony and aspiration, emotion and passion, rejoice and sorrow, love and hatred, belief and betrayal, stress and strain, pollution of mind and environment, splendour of the nature, unexpectable occurrence of the events of the present contemporary society, philosophy of life and death and time and above all scientific thoughts. In the poem 'My Replica' the author elucidates a biological truth about the inheritance of characters in humans generation after generation. The author beholds merrily how his grandson is sleeping calmly, cooly and without any illusion, and thinks intricately the presence of one quarter (25%) of his genes (units of heredity) in the chromosomes (thread-like structures) of each cell of his grandson which also contain the same one quarter of genes of his grandmother. The author also reveals that his son has inherited one half (50%) of his (father's) genes and the other half from his mother's. This process of inheritance continues from one generation to another from the time of origin of modern human beings probably two lakh years ago in Africa and evolved from their most likely recent common ancestor 'Upright man' (in Latin), an extinct species of humans.

    The poem 'Dharmapada' depicts the sacrifice of the life of a twelve year old boy Dharmapada, son of Bishu Mahârana, a great architect, for the sake of twelve hundred stone-masons, engaged for the construction of the Sun Temple at Konark, one of the seven wonders of India, built during the middle 13th century. This anthology of poetry ends with the poem 'Epitaph' in loving memory of the author's elder sister who breathed her last only at the age of three, and his old father and mother who were cremated at Swargadwâra of Puri with a difference of six years, and a young engineer son of his friend who died in the quicksand of a river. The poet is in quest of when, how, why, in which image and at what age death comes ? But no body has yet given the correct answer.

My sincere thanks go to my wife, Vanumati Sahoo, a noted Odia novelist, story-teller and poetess, for her constant encouragement and keen interest in publication of this book. I am thankful to my daughter Dr. Anoja, son Dr. Anubhav, son-in-law Dr. Saiprasad and daughter-in-law Er. Amruta for their goodwill and bless my grandsons Sonu, Paplu, Archis and granddaughter Aura for their interest in their grandfather's and grandmother's books. I am also thankful to the publisher 'Black Eagle Books' for publishing the first international edition of the book decently and timely and taking the task of its international circulation online. Sri Satya Pattanaik, Director of this publishing house and Sri Ashok Parida, its India representative are worthy to be praised for their sincere efforts and keen interest in uplifting and connecting Odia literature globally alongwith Indian and world literature at large. Moreover Mr. Bijay Kumar Mohanty of 'Gudu DTP Art', Cuttack deserves special thanks for its nice type setting. Ultimately I seek the blessings of Lord Ganesh and Goddess Saraswati without whose bliss, the present work would not have been possible. If the poems of this anthology would touch the hearts of the poetry lovers, fruitful will be all my endeavour and effort.

Arun Chandra Sahu

"The butterflies spread their sails
on the sea of light.
Lilies and jasmines surge upon
the crest of the waves of light."
　　　　　　　– *Gitanjali, Rabindranath Tagore*

"In small proportions we just beauties see
And in short measures, life may perfect be."
　　　　　　　– *Ben Johnson*

" I hold it true, whate'er befall;
　I feel it when I sorrow most
　It is better to have loved and lost
Than never to have loved at all."
　　　　　　　– *Alfred Tennyson*

"But, I being poor, have only my dreams;
I have spread my dreams under your feet
Tread softly because you tread on my dreams."
　　　　　　　– *W.B. Yeats*

"Time present and time past
Are both perhaps present in time future,
And time future contained in time past
If all time is eternally present
All time is unredeemable."
　　　　　– *Four Quartets : 'Burnt Norton'*
　　　　　　　　　　- *T.S. Eliot.*

Some Important Stanzas of this poetry collection

'Ultimately metamorphosed surprisingly
into invisible wonderful God particles
laughing millions and millions of times
per second cheerfully'.
                        – The Butterfly of the Cage

'No one wants to quit
but has to quit
at the call of *Yama*
at any time he calculates.'
                        – Travelling Aboard.

'What has He done for us ?
To listen to the cry of a baby
I've already waited fifteen years.'
                        – Conversation with God.

'Here I realized as if
God is hidden in the heart of
Gangasiuli, the queen of the night.'
                        – Existence of God.

'Still in that incompleteness
was filled with completeness
as if of the entire universe.'
                        – Half-crafted Deity.

'Are tears only of pathos and sorrow ?
Isn't it sometimes be of
extreme joyousness ?'
                     – Map of Merriment

'The finest creation of God
is now metamorphosed into *Bhasmâsura.*'
                     – Burning.

'*Veda* says : Rare is human's life,
even rarer are those having knowledge
and rarest are those having poeticness.'
– Even though Superannuated form this Earth.

'Perhaps the treacherous termites
might have hidden that
in their hungry stomach !'
                     – Searching.

'When the Asian openbills
fly in the sky
shed their feathers one by one.
When we walk on the
curvy path of time
shed our melting moments
one by one.'
                     – When the Moon Rises.

'Oh, my dear dreams
minute areas of tiny ships
through my slipping hands, suddenly slip.'
                     – My Dear Dreams.

'Over my back now
I'm dragging loads of
unexpressable griefs
in the narrow snaky road
of endless time.'
                      – Unexpressable

'I'm present, I'm absent.
Birth am I and also birthless.
I'm the rise, I'm the fall,
I'm salvation, I'm damnation,
creation am I and also holocaust.
All the eyes of the universe
on me constantly focus.'
                      – The Indivisible God

'His moments drenched in pathos,
from the eyes of fruits and flowers
of the trees, rolled down tears
in deep despair, the seeds
shattered in the tormented soil.'
                      – The Crab.

'Like Long John Silver
death is walking obliquely here
with one broken leg without fear.'
                      – Death Also Plays Here Holi.

'Will perch a cuckoo on its branch
who would have learnt the art of
laying eggs in its own nest,
will sing romantic songs
for the twelve months a year,
spring would not end there.'
                      – Oath

'However man can easily fly
in darkness, but is burnt
in light in wholeness.'
                    – Disparity

'I'll go up whirling
in the whirl of the smoke
leaving my dear earth
of love and affection
attachment and illusion.'
                    – A lonely Shadow of the Afternoon

'Cladding green sarees
the plants laugh merrily
in rainy season, but tears
roll down from the eyes of the lotus,
being imprisoned by huge water,
a curse to her
though a boon to others.'
                    – Fur of the Bird of Lifespan

'I couldn't guess
which might be unthinkable, unfictionable
undescribable and unbelievable
where infinite universe consisting of
billions and billions of galaxies
are originating from a dot.'
                    – In a Dot

'The leaders will shout
over microphone with grace:
India is progressing ahead
trading the path of hunger and emptiness.'
                    – Guitar

'Also I felt
as if an invisible
sword of Democles
is hanging over my head.'
                     – The Sword of Democles.

'Oh, how these genes are passing
from one generation to another
and from our forefathers !
Behold, how thy genes
are sleeping in tranquility !'
                     – My Replica

'After my death
won't turn down the earth.'
                     – After my Death.

CONTENTS

Prologue	07
The Butterfly of the Cage	29
Travelling Aboard	31
Conversation with God	33
Existence of God	35
Half-Crafted Deity	37
Coming Sunday	39
Vizard	41
Map of Merriment	43
Burning	45
In this Polluted Earth	48
Even though Superannuated from this Earth	50
Searching	52
When the Moon Rises	54
Drenched in the Moonlight	56
My Dear Dreams	58
Distinction	59
Mirror of Senses	61
White Emperor	63
Unexpressable	65
Daughter of 'Swati' Nakshatra	67
Daughter of a Lakh Champak	69
Naughty Laugh	71
The Indivisible God	73
The Crab	75
Death Also Plays Here Holi	78
Life and Death	80
Oath	81

Disparity	84
Question	86
A Lonely Shadow of the Afternoon	88
Will it Happen Such ?	89
Mesmerization	91
In the Mirror of My Eye	93
Magic Stick	95
Two Phases of Sleep	97
Attraction of the Motherland	100
Fur of the Bird of Lifespan	102
The Enchanting Rain	104
Sunstroke in the Rain	106
Donation	107
In a Dot	110
Guitar	112
The Sword of Democles	114
My Replica	116
Suicide of the Murderer	118
Full stop	120
Dharmapada	122
After My Death	124
Immersion of My Bone	126
Invitation of Death	128
Epitaph	130

The Butterfly of the Cage

One day I visualized instantaneously
the cage was open and empty
flown away the bird forever.
Again I closed and locked
the cage conscientiously.

>After some days I saw
>a caterpillar in the cage
>had spun a silky cocoon
>of art of state.
>Emerged from it after a few days
>a number of tiny butterflies.

Crawling over the graveyard
of the mother butterfly
they flew to the crushed sky
by their miniature wings,
licked the blueness of the sky,
snatching various colours
from the multicoloured clouds
painted their wings gorgeously.
From the flowers of little dazzling stars
sucked honey to their hearts' content,

roamed in pairs in the
baffled iron garden
and raised their offspring
with the passage of time.

    Generation after generation
    the number of butterflies enhanced,
    no space was left in the cage
    to freely flutter their wings.
    Gradually transformed the butterflies
    into winged termites,
    in the next generation into ants and flies,
    in the subsequent generation
    into bacteria and viruses.

Ultimately metamorphosed surprisingly
into invisible wonderful God particles*
laughing millions and millions of times
per second cheerfully.

■

*God particle : It is the nick name of Higgs Boson particle, a subatomic particle of the universe and the 2013 Nobel prize in Physics was awarded for its discovery. It is also called so after the 1993 book, 'The God Particle' by Nobel laureate Leon Lederman. Higgs Boson particle is partly named after an Indian scientist S. N. Bose who worked with Albert Einstein.

Travelling Aboard

Old sweet memories
peeped into my mind
on my travelling aboard
a decade ago.
    The thrilling silhouette
    of the sunset
    in the remote village in Switzerland,
    the gorgeous pyramidal peak
    of Matterhorn mountain,
    with the surreal beauty
    of a movie set
    nature crafted New Zealand
    sparkling with snow-capped peaks,
    coastal glaciers, fjords
    and rain forest land
    all mesmerized me.
The wonderful mist flow
on boat in Niagara falls
and the startling green coloured water
of the Niagara river,
the magnificent sky scraper
of Burj Khalifa in Dubai,
the world's tallest man-made architecture
enchanted me forever.

Sitting thoughtfully
on the bank of the River Thames
the picturesque London Bridge,
the colossal copper Statue of Liberty
of New York, the charismatic
river basin of Mississipe,
the second longest river
of North America,
the amazing biodiversity
of the tropical rain forests of Amazon
all roamed me in the sky of elation.
My mind flied to the
orchards of the Netherlands
to feel the pleasure of
plucking ripe cherry, strawberry,
gooseberry, blackberry and red berry,
the elegant boulevards of the
urban landscape of Paris,
the fashionable seaside resorts
of the Côte d'Azar in France
with the modern emblem of the
Eiffel Tower and the attractive
Elephant Palace of Versailles.
   A galaxy of worders
treasures our lovely earth.
No one wants to quit it
but has to quit
at the call of *Yama*
at any time he calculates.

Conversation with God

I was surprised receiving
SMS from God
to chat with Him at mid night
at twelve o'clock twelve minutes.
Very secret matter He will inform me
of course mentioned at last
one million rupees per minute!
    From where shall I collect
    so much money to chat with Him today?
    Given me instruction
    only to chat at that specified time
    which will transform me strangely
    and amazingly to climax
    that I would not have dreamt
    in my life time.
Hesitating I was
to inform it to my better-half
who was preparing paneer biryani
I couldn't resist to tell her.
Being irritated said she :
Why are you disturbing me
when I am preparing a nice dish?
Instead, I went on telling about God's message.
Furiously shouted she : Oh no!

Don't tell me about God or Fod ?
What has He done for us ?
To listen to the cry of a baby
I've already waited fifteen years!
But in vain !
    However, knowing the amount per minute
    I felt, as if she'll faint.
    With a melancholy voice remarked she :
    My darling, have you purchased
    a diamond necklace for me uptill now ?
    Very shrewd is He like *Krishna*.
    Playing on a flute, mesmerizing you
    so much money He'll take away
    that you wouldn't have earned
    in your life time !
    He willn't leave you
    before transforming you
    to a beggar to play on a flute
    from street to street.
    Are you listening to me
    oh, my dear !
On that night goddess of sleep
was not coming to my eyes.
All of a sudden, a ring tone
buzzed in my mobile.
Anxiously I saw
it's nobody else than God.
In dilemma, I pressed
the switch off button,
at that time my wife
was snoring in a deep sleep.

■

Existence of God

Through the railing of my window
rose the sun amidst the morning
chilled mist.
Rubbing my eyes
I woke up from the bed of darkness,
stood near the window,
looked drowsily at the Aurokaria tree
that has stood proudly
throughout the night without sleep,
stretching its hands all around
in the centre of the faithful garden.
On its green branch had perched
a lovely little bird.
How splendorous were her wings
with multicoloured glazed feathers
and awesome mien ?
Singing melodious songs
that can touch any body's heart.
The existence of God
here I realized.
     Yesterday when the dark night was in
     slumber,
     at once I woke up.
     A sweet smell coming through

the window thrilled my heart,
in bewilderment I peeped through the
window.
Oh! it's the brilliant flowers
of *Gangasiuli*, the tree of sorrow, the coral
Jasmine
making us delight by emitting
sweet fragrance in the darkness of night.
Though before dawn will shed
the organge–stalked white flowers,
still is perfect its short span of life
of one night only.
Here I realized as if
God is hidden in the heart
of *Gangasiuli*, the queen of night.

Half-Crafted Deity

While composing poems during midnight
calmly sat God by my side.
    While I was knitting flowers of words
    with various colours of the rainbow
    over a white bedspread,
    he was indicating
    to compose in a particular way
    to pluck that metaphor from heaven,
    not perfect this line
    transform it with that image,
    set this precious word
    in the heart of the poem
    and many alterations
    that are confidential amongst
    both of us.
From the sky
the dazzling stars were going to be faded
while my poem was also going to be completed.
But something more was
to compose, I perceived,
as if it was half-built
just like the half-crafted deity
when queen Gundichâ* opened the door.
    Throughout the home I searched

>   where had gone God
>   to give me final instruction
>   for completion of the long poem ?
> But alas !
> nowhere God was found
> just like the vanishing of the old carpenter.
>   Still in that incompleteness
>   was filled with completeness
>   as if of the entire universe.

* Gundichâ : She is the aunt of Lord Jagannath to whom he visits with his siblings annually during car festival at Puri.

Coming Sunday

Not equal is each Sunday,
but this Sunday is approaching
with a super package of very special dreams.
   Coming Sunday morning is there
plantation programme
amongst Minister of Forests at Jayadev Vatika,
distribution of clothes at Kasturaba shelter home,
as a resource person at Jayadev Bhawan
in the International Seminar on
'Environmental Pollution',
to attend Mrs.Ahulahulia's lunch party
along with my better half,
otherwise compassionate desires
won't swim in the pool of delite.

Coming Sunday evening is also packed with
dinner party of Mr. Mahapatra's farewell ceremony
at May Fair Lagoon.
  Listening to the ghazal of pathos,
shedding drops of crocodile tears
with facial bewilderness
will have to swipe the face of time
with perfumed handkerchief.

Visualizing the anxious and jubilant face
in the obedient mirror,
I'll have to fight with the fragile dreams
in the war field,
to lay down on the arrow-bed like *Bhishma*[*].
A special Sunday is coming this time
with a chameleon face
to play hide-and-seek with day and night dreams.

■

[*] *Bhishma*: A legendary figure in 'Mahâbhârata', who laid down on a bed of arrows for fifty-eight days after falling in the war on the 10th day.

Vizard

Cladding the veil of selfishness
many renowned personalities
from different strata of life
are acting awefully
in the diversified stages
of dissected India.
Secretly weeping Mother India,
who is coming forward
to swipe her tears ?
    Crocodile tears in their outer faces,
    but inside, the ramified roots
    they destroy and snatch away
    the invaluable gems and ornaments
    from the treasury of common man
    heaping in the magnificent
    bungalows and Swiss banks.
    Naked truth of the time.
In the creamy tender bed
of air-conditioned gorgeous suite,
even though taking foreign champagne
sip by sip
still there's no sleep
anxiety has penetrated very deep.
    Eating raw preparation of mango kernel,

drinking a glass of raw liquor of *Mahuli*
Lakhan Marandi sleeps without tension
on the torn cotton clothes,
in a remote village,
snores briskfully, dreaming as if
he is adorning the royal throne
of a renowned state,
attending him a group of subordinates,
some are fanning him with chowries*.
Before the royal audience of ministers
and lords, he is ordering :
Unveil the vizards of all prisoners
and royal men,
I will visualize one after another,
whether all are looking like
real human beings loyal to my state
or bizarre demons of an alien land !

■

* Chowries (singular : chowry) : fly-flappers or whisks originally made from the bushy tails of yaks.

Map of Merriment

Unmeasurable is the hidden
sea of tears in my eyes
but extremely less than it
is seen externally faintly
as a portrait of splendour.
    Are tears only of pathos and sorrow!
    Isn't it sometimes be
    of extreme joyousness!
    That is seen suddenly in the sea
    like a very tiny boat
    and vanishing abruptly
    in the horizon of my
    diminishing life span!
My map of merriment
you've drowned
in the sea of sorrows.
How shall I get it
by searching the vast sprawling water
of the sea!
How many times shall I throw
the net of credence
standing on the shore of infidelity?
    Pacified my heart going to be broken
    in the invisible storm.

No doubt, one day will return the sea
my portrait that does not drench in water
bound with unrotten wooden frame
while the star *Swati* will be in the night sky
and drops of rain water
falling on a lucky oyster,
there will take birth
a highly priced dazzling pearl.

■

Burning

Oblation is continuing
burning of the sacred wood
in the altar of devotion.
Time and again pure ghee is poured,
flame of the fire is ascending up,
in the air is whirling
the pleasant smell of the burnt ghee
cleansing the environment making it pious and
germfree,
drops of water will be born from burning.
In the sky will roam
clouds of aspiration.

    Burning in the stomach
    of a hungry man
    honestly he is begging.
    He who gives him cooked rice
    in his own hand with love and affection
    to pacify his hunger
    will no doubtly get heavenly pleasure.

For a long distance
is burning the jungle
in the hot summer.

No escape for the foliage and animals.
To far-off places
the birds are flying away.
By howling and uproaring
the four-footed animals are running away.
The red angry flame
is tanning the face of the moon
in the night sky,
shedding warm tears the stars
become gloomy and lustreless.

    Extremely high is the burning of mind
    which nobody can visualize.
    Into pieces it dissects your life
    fried with torment
    your every moment,
    the world tastes bitter.
    To get rid of this
    needs His blessings.

In the earth now
the burning is enhancing at a geometric rate.
Year after year
polluted, poisoned
and warmed is the atmosphere.
Time will come
from the north and south pole
ice bergs will flow and dance
on the equator.
The humans will surely engulf

the man-made poisoned fruit
of imprudence and there will be
a universal cataclysm.
    The finest creation of God
    is now metamorphosed
    into *Bhasmâsura**.

* *Bhasmâsura*: The self-destroying demon.

In This Polluted Earth

On the floor of this scared earth
I am sleeping inside
the shell of unbelief
closing my hands and legs of belief
like a frightened tortoise
sleeping inside its carapace
calmly closing its legs.

>So many wars have occurred
>over this floor for centuries
>to obtain a drop of *Amrit*,
>the divine elixir.
>The war may be
>between the friendly parties
>or between the rival parties,
>may be between both the parties
>When they have shown
>white flags extending
>up to the blue sky, peace may prevail.

Of course, first will die
the soldiers in the war,
then the deputy commander,
joint commander and lastly the commander,

but ultimately will accept the defeat
the army chief claded with false vanity
who believes the world
as his own.

> He who gets a drop of *Amrit*
> and sallows it hurriedly,
> will be metamorphosed
> to a demon as all the
> divine properties of it
> have lean altered to evil properties
> in the arena of this
> polluted earth !

■

Even though Superannuated from this Earth

In this ripe old age, I thought
I couldn't compose poems.
    In this age
    the name of God only one has to utter,
    the time I am spending
    in movement of any hands and legs
    should be spent
    in worshiping Him
    that would be added
    in the pages of virtue of my book of fate
    which would help me
    keeping well in my next life
    which, not at all, I would know
    once I enter my graveyard !
However, *Veda** says:
Rare is human's life
even rarer are those having knowledge
And rarest are those having poeticness.
    Day and night can anybody spend
    in worshiping God
    can easily utter his name
    after eating to one's heart's content

and sitting comfortably.
Decided, therefore, I had,
lest God may think otherwise,
on the branch of tree of poeticness
I'll sit.
Those juicy fruits of it
that I have taken thoughout my life
shall I return one by one
which will be sewed into a garland
that will dazzle like a pearl-garland,
even though I am superannuated
from this lovely and lively earth.

* *Veda*: Vedas are four, composed in Vedic Sanskrit, are religious poetry texts of Hinduism originated in ancient India, consisting of 20,379 mantras.

Searching

When searching for an important file
surprisingly a diamond ring I found
from a dilapilated corner of the room
which I could recognize easily
that I had presented you
after the union of
our four eyes.
        In your lovely finger
        was dazzling
        that diamond ring magnificently.
        How fortunate was that ring
        to feel the warmth of your
        soft and tender finger
        below the glossy skin of which
        was circulating germ-free blood
        of your love.
But when your blood was filled
with germs of detestation
and your faithful shadow disappeared
I couldn't know at all.
        I searched you ardently
        in the streets, shops, markets,
        villages and towns, rivers and streams
        jungles and waterfalls

and the long sea shore.
But in vain.
If I'll go straight
either in east or west direction
I'll come back again
to the same place where I have started
as the earth is round.
May it take eighty days
like the French author Jules Verne's character
or may it be eighty months
or eighty years (of course if my inhale and exhale
cooperate me).
Still, I could not visualize
the champak bud- like fingers of yours,
could not feel the existence
of your warm inhale and exhale
or tinkling sound of your heart.
Only the twinkling of the stars
I could see in the black sky.
All my hopes and aspirations I lost
and raised my hands upwards.
    Gone are those days,
    but today, in the lazy afternoon
    of Sunday, bit by bit
    I'm searching the very important
    document, but could not find
    amidst the heaps of haggard files
    and stacks of bleached books.
    Perhaps the treacherous termites
    might have hidden that
    in their hungry stomach !

When the Moon Rises

When the moon rises
in the virgin sky of the mind
wings of poets proliferate eventually.
They start flying
to guzzle the bewildered moonlight
to their hearts' content.

    However, for six months,
    the Eskimos can't
    visualize the moon.
    Wearing skin dresses of pathos
    they sleep in the egloos of aspiration
    dreaming the damsel of separation.
    Oh, when'll the moon come again
    showing her tranquilizing face ?

In the deep dark sky
when the pregnant clouds of ambition
float rapidly, the darlings come out gleefully
wearing swimming suits
to dive in the romantic water
of the lover rain.

When the stars twinkle
in the somnolent sky
the male and female doves
dream romantic dreams
and coo sweetly
in the calm midnight.

When the Asian openbills
fly in the sky
shed their feathers one by one.
When we walk on the
curvy path of time
shed our melting moments
one by one.

Drenched in the Moonlight

In the veins and veinlets of green leaves
flows an impeccable freshness,
a primeval greenness.
Nobody knows when it appeared exactly,
most probably a hundred million years ago.

    A storehouse of unbelievable
    quality of your heartly love,
    what I felt.
    By throwing the shedded flowers
    of envy, agony and pride
    in the deep womb of river water
    collected gold sands of love and affection
    from the desireless river beds
    to prepare a necklace of the rainbow
    for your metaphysical neck.

Mixed in my blood of blue veins
the juices of neem flowers and bitter leaves,
poured the colours of red rose petals
in the blood of my red arteries,
which tear buttons from my shirt
inflicted by the temporary excitement.

Varied shades of colours
of the primitiveness
appear from time immemorial.
Drenched in the moonlight
of the defamed moon
the footprints of modernness
fading away with the
passage of eternal time.

My Dear Dreams

Hidden are bitter griefs
in deep dark lonely caves.
Sometimes peep from that cave
thirsty dreams in anxiety
to drink dew drops of desire
in early hours of winter morning,
while dropping from the drowsy grasses
the dews look like precious pearls
in the morning sun rays.
    In grief and agony
    sorrows shed tears in streams
    over the shining hot sands
    of the cursed desert.
    Branches and cherries of date palm
    cover them completely
    being flown from distant oasis
    by dust devils.
Oh, my dear sorrows
sprawling water of the blue sea
touching the limitless sky !
Oh, my dear dreams
minute areas of tiny ships
through my slippery hands, suddenly slip !

Distinction

Time of happiness
mingles within a moment
like a water bubble.

    Time of sorrowfulness
    floats like a dried leaf
    in the speedy stream of
    curvy river of life
    facing boldly all the adverse situations.
    Marches ahead on and on
    encountering the ups and downs
    thorns and prickles of life.

Even if stones fall from the temple,
thousands of trees are cut
from the *Sipa Sarubâli*,
even if are closed the digging of mines and
minerals,
bail is granted to Salman Khan,
even if acquitted the political leader
from the corruption of billions of money,
even if thousands of humans
die in sunstroke
still the stream marches ahead

till it mingles within the womb of blue sea
where congregate millions and billions
of water bubbles
which demise infinitely in a moment,
and are created infinitely in the next moment.

∎

Mirror of Senses

You can see me
to your heart's content
in the mirror of sense of visualization.

> Can focus light of rainbow colours
> on my entire body
> time and again
> but can't touch me.
> Order of the king:
> if you touch
> you will be made senseless
> by cruel torture.
> After getting sense,
> will be surprised to know
> a fine of one hundred gold cions,
> if can't pay
> one month's rigorous imprisonment.

Of course, for somebody it may be
like only one gold coin
but for others it may be
like one crore of gold coins.

Saying that content you are
with the amount of coin you get,
on its truth one may apprehend.
Are all become Buddha !
Can all shatter desire !
If all become fakirs
who will be there in the villages
to give them alms ?

I am only incarnation
of senses of visualization,
be content with that only.
Oh offender !
meditate for years
to attain my sense of touch.

But the mirror of the
modern society
reflects the enjoyment
of any kind of sense !

White Emperor

In the full moon sky of January
was laughing the moon whitely,
wearing white dresses
spreading were the white clouds
towards the white horizon.
Shinning brilliantly your alluring face
with the white rays of the full moon.
As if remaining in an alien state,
you were gazing without blinking
at the silvery moon, oh my dear !

    All of a sudden
    rolled down white tears
    from the eyes of the moon
    rolled down white blood
    from her enchanting body
    looked white her cries.
    Tonnes and tonnes of griefs
    congregate like a hill
    upon which were heaps of
    white ashes.
    Inside it were smiling or crying
    enigmatically white lilies in an illusionism,
    ask Mona Lisa !

In the crystal-clear pond
staring are the fishes in their still silvery eyes
at the blackspot of the moon,
but covered it a gushing white cloud.
    In the realm of moon
    white is the love,
    white is severance
    white is also rendezvous
    white is betrayal as well,
    moreover, white is the birth and life
    death too is white !
In the white empire of endless sky
moon is the only white emperor,
adorned with white royal robes
emitting white aura.

■

Uexpressable

As a token of love
at first sight, when I put
a diamond ring in your finger,
oh, my dear !
you looked like an angel
of the fairy kingdom, I'm sure.

    The glaze of your face
    dazzled the surrounding,
    passed amazingly sparkling waves
    in my entire body and mind.
    Roaming was a hypnosis of engrossment
    at the speed of lightning
    from land to sky.

All of a sudden you told
one day: That diamond ring
was lost somewhere that I couldn't know,
extremely sorry oh my dear !

    I searched for it
    every corner of the earth
    from sea shore to horizon,
    but alas! could not get

any clue of its finding,
lest that might have been mingled
in the carbon molecules of darkness !
Thought I, let the ring
be not found, but you remain
by my side as a faithful shadow
like the presence of *Arundhati*
close to *Vashistha* in the *Saptarishi* constellation.
But you would be lost one day
was out of my imagination.
It was in vain, to search for you.
Enhanced many time my tension
in the post-mortem of probing.
Over my back now
I am dragging
loads of unexpressable griefs
on the narrow snaky path
of endless time.

Daughter of *'Swati'* Nakshatra

Smoothly she was born
without caesarean operation
when there was *lagna* (ascendant)
of *'Swati'* Nakshatra,
laughing was the morning star
in the east horizon.
    Tender rays of the morning sun
    were getting ready to come,
    while flying and flying
    the birds were merrily singing.
    In the first cry of the baby
    shattered was the anxiety,
    smile appeared in the lips
    of parents, rolled down
    from their eyes tears of happiness.
In such a priceless moment
when *'Swati'* constellation is there
and if rain drops fall,
rarely and secretly takes birth
a musk in the naval
of a deer in the forest,
pearl in the womb of an oyster in the sea
and black pearl in the head of a cobra
in a hidden place of the mountain.

In such an auspicious moment
was she born
like the musk of the deer,
pearl of the oyster or elephant
or *gorâchanâ*, the cow stone.
That was Thursday,
the tenth lunar day, the day of
observance of *Sudashâbrata* and *Bâhudâ*,
the return day of car festival,
heavy crowd of devotees at Puri.
All holy events congregated on that lucky day,
the baby daughter would have a lucky fate.
Growing she was day by day
like the enhancement of new moon's shape
increasing also was
her glow with time.
He who was beholding her,
commenting :
She has a flawless beauty.
    Said the astrologer:
    She will be an all-round scholar,
very efficient in medical science.
He who would have excellence in study,
knowledge
and intelligence and fate in high position
would be her life mate.
My forecast will not be in vain.

■

Daughter of a Lakh Champak

That was a full moon day of June.
Lord Jagannath, Balabhadra
and Devi Subhadra were bathing
by one hundred eight pots
of holy water in Srikhetra, Puri.
Blue sea on the other side
and sea of people on this side.
The anxiety of devotes was enhancing
from time to time.

>On that auspicious day
>early in the morning
>she was born.
>The young sun was eager to see her.
>The black clouds were laden with rain drops.
>Came to an end all anxieties
>after the birth of a daughter, a gem,
>in the cradle place of a remote village.

Every day she was feeding
with orange juice, taking bath
with lukewarm water of love and affection,
sleeping calmly with mosquito-net cover.
Day by day was enhancing

her beauty with lusture.
She was the apple of the eye
of all including grandfather and grandmother,
showered her with blessings of their souls.

    Nobody was like her
    in beauty, knowledge, education,
    nature, respect and devotion.
    Telling once the grandmother:
    He who would offer
    a lakh champak flowers
    over the head of Lord Shiva
    with extreme concentration and devotion
    and would have remained
    at the climax of glory
    would hold her hand
    and be her life-partner
    for all time to come.

Who's that lucky partner ?
Am I ?

Naughty Laugh

In this rainy night
you are really remembered very much
I can't sleep tight.

> Birds of my desire
> with their wings of aspiration
> fly to your nest
> to rub their cold beaks
> with the warm beak of yours.
> But being drenched in rain
> you eagerly wait
> for my faithful path.

However, in telepathy, I come
you welcome me, embrace me,
kiss me exotically.
In your eyes
moonlight of a thousand moon,
in your lips
bewildered scent of a lakh champak,
in your dreams
lusture of a million *Airavata*.*

All of a sudden
in a dreadful thunder
you clasp me very tightly,
extreme tightly for a long time
like the statue of Ajanta and Elora.
I catechize:
Are you really fear
such thunder sound
of the naughty rain ?

But in your eyes
appears a naughty laugh !

■

* *Airavata*: The mythological winged white elephant who carries Lord *Indra,* the God of gods.

The Indivisible God

Addition am I,
subtraction am I,
arithmetic am I,
I'm also dividend and divisor,
quotient and remainder
I'm also zero.
Division of zero by zero is infinite
which am I, I'm *mahasunya*,
the extreme voidness.
Division of *mahasunya* by *mahasunya*,
is extreme infinite
which I'm.

> Visible am I and invisible.
> obtrusive am I and also unobtrusive.
> Eternal am I and also perpetual.
> I'm all tangible and intangible
> happiness and prosperity,
> pathos and pain
> inexhaustible storehouse
> of all those mind power.

I'm present, I'm absent.
Birth am I and also birthless.

I'm the rise, I'm the fall,
I'm salvation, I'm damnation,
creation am I and also holocaust.
All the eyes of the universe
on me constantly focus.
Am I indivisible God ?

The Crab

How elegantly the crab
is running over the muddy soil !
Then hided inside a hole
and came out after sometime,
ran and suddenly attacked
and trapped a small creature,
greed of consumer over the prey.

    How hiddenly came the
    notorious cancer ?
    In which way,
    at which time arrived silently
    no body could find its sign.
    Entered and trapped his liver,
    enlarged it more and more
    sent from that area
    deadly missiles to different
    organs of the body
    to capture for all time to come
    to alter their geography.

To nullity the missiles
sent by the carcer
tried their best many radiations and chemicals.

In this war, roared the sky with cracking,
flame of the fire was burning
higher and higher with radiant rays.
Created hurricane also the wind,
being transformed to hailstones
water also attacked.
Thrilled melancholy
the flesh and bone
of shattered earth.

    The age was not so high.
    In the soft rays of the afternoon
    were playing hide and seek
    the leaves of the trees
    with the naughty wind.
    The sun had not yet set in the west.
    Goddess evening had not been stepped
    to worship in the temple of the earth.
    To make people thrilled and bewildered
    night had not come with starry darkness.

Gradually the graph of his agony
rose high; his moments drenched in pathos.
From the eyes of fruits and flowers
of the tress rolled down tears.
In deep despair the seeds
shattered on the tormented soil.
The young seedlings germinated
few days back knew nothing about the world,
still stopped their playing
and caressed his face and backside.

The birds sitting before on the trees
returned shortening their foreign tours
hearing the sad news
from the very speedy wind.
How good was the noble man !
Was taking much care of ours
extending a helping hand in our troubles.
What can we do
in such a pathetic situation ?
Only we can pray:
Oh God !
Let his soul be mingled with *Paramâtmâ*.

Death Also Plays Here *Holi*

Like Long John Silver
death is walking obliquely here
with one broken leg, without fear.
For how many years
will he work here
like a slave ?

> In a triangular forest
> present at the angle of sixty degree
> a magnificent tree in whose
> small cave, building a nest
> a bird has slept.
> Sitting by his side
> a female bird is twittering
> with a different tune with pauses.

In the solitude of the dense forest
whether that tune is of love,
or terror or of death ?

> Invisible are the rickshaws
> in the new crowed city,
> the lyrics of the rickshawalas have vanished.
> In the lighted streets of darkness

the lady sellers paint the blood
of innocent fish on the chopper,
move their finger tips
on the touchscreen of smartphones.

Death also plays here *Holi*
at noon in the crowded market place.
All are spectators,
no one is a saviour.

Life and Death

Don't go to the city,
fair is there of covered cadavers.
Dreadful shadow of extreme terror
is hovering over the lanes,
streets and market places.

    Crowds in the hospitals,
    crowds in the nursing homes,
    quarrelling with the
    representatives of death
    pale yellow faces of agony.
    But undone they are.
    Strict order has come.
    As if vapourised the pityness.

Erotic dancing of the viruses
has been enhancing with time.
Tricks for shattering the enemies
are the main aim of the time.
Hide and seek of life and death
is now the scene of the time.

Oath

Taken oath we've:
The deeds we did not perform
in our previous life
will be fulfilled in this life.

> Taken oath by witness of fire,
> by witness of priest
> who while offering ghee
> in *homa* was chanting hymns
> keeping the mobile close to his ear;
> also including our near and dear ones
> and wellwishers as witnesses
> who were showering flowers
> gazing constantly towards us.

According to our oath
we will construct first
a very big house,
not house but a bungalow.
By bricks and cements
of love and affection
will be built its walls,
by steel-rods of faith its roof.
With non-salinized blue sea water

of aspiration will be filled
the dazzling bath tubs
and our dreams with angels
will swim exotically,
hanging the helium balloons of time
in the most attractive drawing room.

> Brining a *Pârijâta* (*Magnolia*) tree from
> heaven
> we'll plant in our garden
> in the south west corner,
> pour water of affection
> for its luxuriant growth.
> Will perch a cuckoo on its branch
> who would have learnt the art of
> laying eggs in its own nest,
> will sing romantic songs
> for twelve months of a year
> spring would not end there.

We'll fetch multicoloured fishes,
train them the tricks of swimming
according to our own will
in a ten-feet aquarium.

> Many other deeds
> will be performed as per the
> instruction of our souls,
> that we could not perform
> in our previous life.

Is it necessary to give
detailed accounts to all ?
He who opt to know is knowing.
Will we declar
so much secret matter
limited between us ?

■

Disparity

While going to worship
wearing trouser and punjabi,
a notorious house fly sat on the
golden button of the punjabi.

    Is there any hindrance for the house fly
    after roaming in nasty drains
    to come again to sit
    on this golden coloured button ?
    An unwritten right is there
    for the flies to sit on any thing
    of the world,
    may it be living or dead
    fresh or rotton !

While worshiping the god
all of a sudden sat the house fly
on the nose of a god,
looking like a black spot.
Tried to drive away the house fly
but it sat on the sweet *bhog*.
Will god take the sweet
dreaded by the legs of the house fly
containing millions of germs ?

Undone I became
before a mere house fly,
raised my hands to the blank sky.

> Closed the doors and windows,
> lest the house fly hating the darkness
> may fly out to light
> through any small hole.

However, man can easily fly
in darkness,
but is burnt in light
in wholeness.

Question

In the hell is my legs
in the heaven is my head
in the earth is rest of my body.

    Various kinds of birds aimlessly fly
    in the pale dark endless sky.
    Fire balls are running everywhere speedily,
    the tips of the guns
    are following them secretly.

    In today's night
    after the entire earth sleeps
    in deep slumber,
    a procession of headless torsos
    will come exactly at two thirty.

The night will continue,
the sun will be hidden
in an invisible cave of a magician
for days seven.

    Only night and night
    will be this week,
    heaven for the nocturnals,

hell for the day rovers,
mortal earth for the evening roamers.

Am I a miraculous creature
of the heaven, hell
and the mortal earth ?

A Lonely Shadow of the Afternoon

I'm a lonely shadow
of the diminishing afternoon
slowly elongating
to touch the *Swargadwâra* of Puri.

    When the night is too deep
    the dreadful roaring of the sea
    is only heard,
    invisible the horizon of the night
    mingling both the sky and sea
    like the mingling of the soul
    with the God,
    at that time gradually
    I'll go up whirling
    in the whirl of the smoke
    leaving my dear earth
    of love and affection,
    attachment and illusion.

■

Will it Happen Such ?

Will it happen such that
by the grace of God, we would
take birth two times
in this exact figures of ours !

    In this life
    we become husband and wife
    from lover and beloved.
    Facing the visible dark
    and invisible light of the world
    we have or haven't become
    steady intellects.
    Still, we have germinated
    two seeds, made them grow luxuriantly
    by watering and supplying nutrients.
    How beautiful leaves
    have imerged from them !
    Scented flowers will blossom,
    laden with juicy fruits,
    our dreams will come true.

I'll take birth again
in my next life
in the same house of my village

in the same cradle place.
You'll also take birth
in your same cradle place,
just after four years
four months and four days
of my next birth.
    In the next life
    we'll have the similar figure
    and will be jubilant young
    like the present life
    assimilating the air and water of the earth.
    Again, we'll sit
    in the marriage mandap
    the priest will make knot
    in our hands.
    You'll whisper:
    You're the same guy
    who was the choice of my mother
    in the last life and became
    my life partner.
    I'll whisper:
    You're the same pretty beauty
    out of a lakh,
    who was also my darling
    and life partner
    in my previous life.
Let our lives continue together
for generation after generation.
Oh, Lord of the heaven !

Mesmerization

Swimming over the sea of the sky
the wandering winds
unveiled the saree of the cloud and
the face of the moon became glaring.
How beautiful was the moon
like a dazzling diamond
in the darkness ?
But alas !
blackness of blemish
someone has rubbed in her face
for all time to come !
In shame she has bowed down
her face and has drawn
some indicative lines
on the sand of the sea
like a difficult diagram of geometry.

    When in the sky
    was the fourth lunar moon
    I unveiled your red veil
    glittered your moon-like face
    but you became shy
    like the droopping of the creepers
    under hot sun.

Moving your eye balls
like a deer, looking downwards
drew on the sand of time
invisible art of passion
by your champak fingers.
Whirling around you
a sweet smell of champak
mesmerized me wholly.
Pulled again your veil of passion
lest I might not tolerate
so much of mesmerization.

All at once, came gushing
the naughty wind
covered the face of the moon
by the veil of the proud cloud.

■

In the Mirror of My Eye

When you get angry,
oh my dear
vanish from you face all fear !
As if all your senses
co-operate perfectly.
I laugh gaily
but my blood becomes snow.
    Without any expression
    in your face
    you express:
    Is my becoming angry
    really an act of exhibiting anger ?
    I'am angry with you
    because I love you very much.
    Am I furious like a fireball
    with Tom, Harry and Dick ?
    My temperament
    how couldn't you understand?
Thought I, you are right,
your anger is an expression
of your intense love.
Like that as I love you to the moon and back
can't I angry with you
keeping all my senses alert ?

> Then I get angry with you
> so much that
> streams of wayward tears
> rolled down from your pretty eyes.
> Sobbingly you uttered :
> You don't love me at all,
> otherwise how do you outrage so much
> instead to lull ?

I told:
Oh no, just as you become angry
by loving me, I'm furious with you more
by loving you more.

> Vanished quickly tears from your eyes
> in the next moment,
> a charming smile pepped instead
> that entered the mirror of my eyes
> at the speed of lightning,
> suddenly I embraced you warmly,
> and also you.

∎

Magic Stick

With pointed blue-polished nails
you pressed my palm so tightly
that swelled up to the sky.

> Then I pressed your apple cheek
> time and again,
> but oozed blood from my fingers
> like streams in your
> invisible tender body
> which you tried to obstacle
> by bridging between two hills,
> lest that bridge would be
> filled with my warm fresh red blood
> where blue whales would swim
> up and down, down and up
> blowing blood upwards
> through their eyes.

You patted slowly backside
of my lifespan that was diminishing
but I felt as if
it was enhancing gradually !
> To enhance your lifespan
> to place the time at your youth

I touched my magic stick
from your hand to toe,
that was presented by my forefathers
in my previous life.
■

Two Phases of Sleep

By research has proved one psychologist:
Long ago when there was no lamp or electricity
people used to sleep
in two phases at night.

    After sunset
    when darkness covered the earth
    nothing to do in dark,
    like the birds
    taking dinner people used to sleep
    after evening in deep sleep
    in the first phase
    up to midnight.
    Then people woke up for some time
    thinking what could be done
    for the development of his race,
    also, ideal time for reproductive activity
    that would help to continue
    human race generation after generation.

The second phase of sleep
was starting after this
that continued up to the early morning.
Before dawn, people woke up

with full vigour and energy.
After bath and breakfast
used to perform their works.
Sincerely spending their lives
with peace and happiness
without tension or worry
like the birds of the sky.

But behold the condition of modern man !
In the whole earth now
man is full of stress and strain.
Most precious for him is the peace and
contentment at present.
Being entangled with desire and passion
sitting now on the hill of tension
sleeping late of night
after veiwing tv, laptop or tablet
and blue films
for which goddess of sleep
is very annoyed with him.

Let modern man be like a bird,
sleep just after evening,
let his sleep be of two phases
like that of the ancient people.
In between two phases of sleep
he may be engaged in some
creative or reproductive activity
or some other inspiring engagements.
Then only he will ride

the top of the worriless hill
of peace and tranquillity,
would be laughing merrily
the moon and stars
in the clear sprawling sky.

Attraction of the Motherland

The betel vines
are laughing once again
in the land once occupied
by the mining company.

    Will the attraction of motherland
    vanish from one's mind?
    He will struggle and fight
    for his own right,
    let blood may ooze
    from his skeletal body.

In this motherland
generation after generation
have passed smoothly.
The sun laughs here in the day
and the moon pours
millions of dreams at night.
Hide and seek play here
the rain, spring and summer.
With radiant clouds and breezy wind
all events pass here harmoniously.

Where from did come this company ?
Made conspiracy secretly with the
government,
destroyed hundreds of betel vines.
Rice fields became barren lands,
paralysed the livelihood of people
upset was the boat of life.
All the arrows of tears and blood
they hit were vanished
in the mesmerization of the company.

Still a ray of hope has emerged now
lest the foreign company
may quit this land.
Again, they will hug
their motherland with love and affection
and their lives will be
again vibrant and jubilant.

Fur of the Bird of Lifespan

Cladding green sarees
the plants laugh merrily
in rainy season, but tears
roll down from the eyes of the lotus
being imprisoned by huge water,
a curse to her,
though a boon to others.
Sun god is aggrieved
by not visualizing the beautiful face
of the lotus.
Behold, the courage of the
ordinary clouds, making abatable
in the path of the sun !

      Heavy rain was there yesterday night.
      Falling on the leaves of banana
      the rain drops were making
      a rhythmical music
      that touched my heart with delight.
      The loving face of my beloved
      peeped in the sky of my mind.
      Her absence I was feeling very much
      in this exotic rainy night.

Drowsily I was touching smoothly
the red velvet clothes of *Shâdhaba Bohu*[1]
that was dazzling in the
light of the lightning.

    Early in the morning
    someone knocked my door.
    Opened I saw
    cladding the rays of the morning sun
    was standing thy *paramâyu*,[2]
    telling me:
    A fur of the bird of your lifespan
    has fallen in your courtyard
    shattered by last night's heavy rain.

■

---

[1] *Shâdhaba bohu:* Red velvet mites, very eye-catching due to bright redness.

[2] *Paramâyu:* The lifespan of a living being.

The Enchanting Rain

In this rainy night
the earth is vibrating.
Excited are the minds
with galaxy of aspirations.
    The jujube-sized rain drops
    are creating a heart touching rhythm
    of desire, keenness
    and deep anxiousness.
    Drenched in rain,
    drinking *kâdambari*[1]
    are dancing the kadamba flowers
    holding the hands of the wind
    in the radiant light of the lightning
    with the music of thunder,
    dancing with exotic postures
    of *Chausathi Yogini*.[2]

In this rainy night
I remember you passionately, oh my dear !
But alas !
You are far away from here,
alone I'm in this emptied room,
filled with darkness
only me and myself companionless.

My desires are excited
and don't obey me
in this rainy night,
fly away by the strong wind
of aspiration to your hidden place
calmly and quietly.
Amazed you become,
and enquire: How do you know my
address ?
Without caring this stormy night
we've come chasing your
charismatic scented smell.
Fly with us, without you
he is feeling fish out of water.

---

[1] *Kâdambari*: A spirituous liquor distilled from the flower of Kadamba (*Anthocephalus indicus*).

[2] *Chousathi Yogini*: The 64 yoginis are auspicious goddess-like figures and their idols are present in a temple at Hirapur, near Bhubaneswar, which is a tantric shrine. The yogini idols are standing each on an animal, a demon or a human head depicting the victory to Shakti (feminine power). These idols express everything from rage, sadness, pleasure, joy, desire and happiness. Such Yogini temples are present at Ranipur-Jharial site of Bolangir district in Odisha and seven other places in India.

Sunstroke in the Rain

Lover and beloved
become victims to sunstroke
in the rainy season.
    Fetching the colours of the rainbow
    they paste over their entire bodies.
    Drink sip by sip the raindrops
    touching their lips with each other.
    By churning the hailstones
    put in layers over their
    heated heads and chests.
    Clasp each other seeing the lightning,
    the beloved in fear
    but the lover by stinging of ecstasy.
Again it is raining cats and dogs,
touching the bodies with each other
they test wheter the heat of sunstroke
has diminished or not.
Oh no! not at all,
rather if they dance in pairs
under the open sky
drenching in the rain of *kâdambari*
automatically will be reduced
the heatness of the body, mind and heart
and they will fly to a dreamy concourse
in a mall.

Donation

Who will ignore
the supremacy of charity *(dâna)*
amongst *Karmas* ?
    It you donate cooked rice
    to the hungry people
    sitting on the roadside
    diminished will be their hunger,
    will appear rays of contentment
    in their faces.
    Isn't it another name of virtue ?
In the biting cold of winter,
on the roadside the homeless beggars
shrivel inside the torn clothes.
In the midnight
if you go to them and donate
blankets and winter clothes,
with gratitude they will wish you good luck.
It's also a fruit of virtue.
    Who is now donating land?
    All have forgotten
    the *Bhoodân Yagna* of sacrificing land.
    Still if anybody donates land
    to a landless person,
    in his life card will be added

another step of virtue.
'Godan' of Premchand,
is a rare contribution to
Indian literature.
But now, is a rare event,
the donation of cattle.
Still people in the villages
are donating cattle.
Assuredly they will get
the milk of virtue.
    Lifeless is a man without blood.
    A virtuous act is blood donation.
    One may survive from the
    cruel clutches of death by receiving blood
    and he prays God for long life
    of the blood donor.
Splendid achievements
in the arena of medical science
have enhanced the lifespan of humans.
Fear for death may be vanquished,
a damaged organ can be
transplanted with a new one successfully.
Millions of virtues the donor will achieve.
    For the patients
    doctors are the second god.
    Those who render selfless
    health services are praiseworthy,
    virtuous and noble.
From schools to universities
paramount importance is of teachers

in imparting knowledge to the students,
uplift them from darkness
of ignorance to the glowing light of
knowledge and awareness.
The *'Supreme Brahman'* are really the teachers
beyond all descriptions and conceptualization.
None can snatch knowledge
from a knowledgeable person.
The more you teach and preach
the more you become knowledgeable and wise,
in the ladder of success you will rise,
can win the world by virtue of knowledge.
    But in vain all will be
    donating anything to an unworthy person,
    naught will be
    your fruit of virtue.

In a Dot

While searching for you,
you entered a deep dark
large secret hall that I couldn't see you.
I sensed you walking there
like a tributary in a snaky path.
I didn't enter
such a darkened hall before.
From my childhood I knew not
the existence of such a hidden
hall in my premises,
full of dreadful disdain darkness.
    Still, I chased you
    being turmoiled,
    felt as if you entered
    an intense darkened jungle,
    chased you recognizing
    your lotus smell
    that became intense and more intense
    from time to time in darkness.
    Oh, such a mind blowing scent
    I didn't smell from you earlier.
    Did you make a wizardry
    in that deep dark camera !
Cutting the darkness, you marched ahead,

then came a tunnel
that has not seen the sun, but easily you entered
as an expert trader.
I was walking
like a blindman in that deadly tunnel,
only following your sweet scent.
When would be the hungry, heart-thrilling tunnel,
fitted with innumerable dazzling swords
in thy wall, end ?
    What would come next
    one after another
    I couldn't guess,
        which might be unthinkable, unfictionable
        undescribable and unbelievable
        and extreme bliss of infinite universe
        where billions of galaxies
        are originating from a dot.
Oh, my dear !
You're there
in thy dot
and also, I'm.

Guitar

Had I done good or bad
analyzed for some days in this regard.
    Underestimating the time
    as a dormant log
    one day suddenly I invited him
    to pay a visit to my home
    on a particular day
    at a specific time
    as my time and his time
    jointly will have a new discovery.

Really, he came at that particular time
with minimum articles he needed.
Most importantly he brought one guitar
with which he was playing pleasantly
that had attracted me very much.
Of course, I had a guitar previously;
on its strings I was strumming my fingers
the music of *Komal Gândhâr** or
rude *Gândhâr* and one day
the strings were torn.
From that day the chord of my mind
was also torn.

The guitar was lying crumpled
in the corner of a room
like a paralyzed patient.
    However, one has come now
    to strum on the guitar
    with a rhythmic pleasant pitch,
    appeared a ray of happiness
    in my mind.
Stretching my wings, I'll fly
at that time in the blue sky,
or else I will offer him
to drink coconut milk
and its soft tender endosperm
that he likes incredibly
or will offer him
champagne of the heaven.
    Next morning the garbage picker
    may tilt the bottle in his mouth
    lest some drops are left.
    The leaders will shout
    over microphone with grace:
    India is progressing ahead
    trading the path of hunger and emptiness.

∎

* *Komal Gândhâr*: A soft note on a sharp scale.

The Sword of Damocles

Once upon a time
came a distant-related lady
of mine,
    Puzzled she was
    told with submissiveness:
    I'm in untold trouble,
    a hill of tension over my head.
    Will you allow me to stay
    in your house for some days ?
    Then I will go away
    in my own way.

Silent I remained.
Thought she:
Silence is the indication
of confirmation.
Some belonging she had brought
with her; amongst that
was a small black and white puppy.
Of course, I don't like
to keep dogs or don't wish
to stay in a house
where dogs dwell !

Why I remained silent
still I couldn't guess.
Was it the attraction of her beautiful face ?

    Gradually that lady
    spread her kingdom in my house.
    However, I was not feeling easy
    seeing the two eyes of that puppy
    looking like the eyes of a dead fish.
    Perhaps he might have left his mate
    to spend here the life
    of an imprisoned soldier.
    As if an indication
    was given by his two eyes:
    Hanging before him
    a sword of Damocles.

Also, I felt
as if an invisible sword of Damocles
is hanging over my head !

My Replica

My replica I'm visualizing
in the body of my baby grandson.
Closing his lotus eyes,
he has slept on a tender bed
calmly, coolly without any illusion
in a closed posture of hands and legs,
as if *Krishna* has slept
over a baynan leaf
touching his toe in his mouth
with a smiling face.
    In his body is circulating
    my blood and also the blood
    of my forefathers.
    My genes are present in the chromosomes
    of each cell of his body,
    at least by one quarter
    as my son has inherited
    my genes by one half
    and the other half from my better half.
    Oh, how these genes are passing
    from one generation to anther
    and from our forefathers !
    Behold, how thy genes are sleeping
    in tranquility !

I was overhelmed with thought:
Surely God is there,
otherwise, can such a tender, sinless, cute
baby bud be created in the
living kingdom of our earth
amongst the mostly lifeless universe ?

∎

Suicide of the Murderer

How barbarously has the murderer
killed the man !
Ofcourse, ten persons
he has killed before.
At the site assembled people
to see how dreadfully has altered
the geography of that dead man !
      It's a breaking news for all TV channels,
      a hot news for the newspapers,
      still the police has not yet
      traced the murderer,
      but has assigned an award of
      rupees one crore for his head.
Some days passed away
after this brutal event,
passed one month, even one year,
but the tracing was in vain.
Wiped away from the sky
of people's mind this dreadful event.
However, the death anniversary of the dead
was celebrated by his relatives
by hanging garlands of tear drops
in the stage,
offered flower bouquets of anger

to the guests and rebuked
the inefficiency of the government
and the law of the country.
Only they have faith in *Yama,*
the god of truth.
>   Begged energy, vigour, power and bliss
>   from God on that night
>   the successors of that dead man
>   to search and bring that murderer,
>   wound ten times more in his body
>   so that ten tributaries of his blood
>   would flow that would mingle
>   to from a river
>   in whose water of blood
>   if they bathe
>   will rest in peace
>   the soul of the departed man.

All of a sudden one day
a breaking news spread
in TV, radio and newspapers
that the murderer has made suicide
firing his own head
by his own pistol.

Full Stop

We will not fight any more
for this single bedspread
soft and tender.
      Due to its inadequateness,
      a double large colourful bedspread
      you have bought and I have praised
      your choice.
      That can well accommodate a couple
      in this beginning of winter
      in the sweet early morning
      with pleasant cold.
Sweet naughty dreams
in the sweetened early dawn
within the cozy double bedspread,
the dreams feeling cold
calmly pulling the bedspread.
The pleasant lyrics of cuckoo
are also heard inside its warmness.
Oh, through the railings of the window
cool north breeze is pushing
into the glossy bedspread !
      A heap of office works
      is there tomorrow,
      to finalize projects and

to attend important meetings.
All such events entered calmly
into my bedspread,
kicked them and threw them
one after another
out of my gate.
Oh, a very romantic dream
has ridden over me now !
Is it the time
for the calling bell
to ring in a rude voice !
Perhaps the maid servant
has arrived just at six o'clock
shattering all my tantalizing dreams.

■

Dharmapada

The jujube fruits
helped Dharmapada, a twelve year old boy,
to recognize his father,
Bisu Maharanâ, a great architect
of Black Pagoda,
but couldn't check his final decision.
    Ordered the king Lângulâ Narashinga Deva I:
If by tomorrow morning
the top crown of the Sun temple
would not have been completed,
executed would be
all the twelve hundred stone-masons.
Worried all stone-masons including Bisu
as it was not possible
to set the top crown.
But bravo! it was single handedly completed
by Dharmapada in that night,
which could not be performed
by twelve hundred stone-masons!
Which engineering mind had he
at that tender age of twelve years!
Resounded in his mind
the conversation of his father
with his fellow masons:

If the king would know that
a child had done it,
he might beheaded us !
Is it of paramount importance
the lives of twelve hundred masons
or the life of a single twelve-year old boy ?
    Taking final decision, Dharmapada,
    jumped from the top of the temple
    in that fatal dark mid-night
    into the blue water of Chandrabhâgâ,
    scarified his life at the cost of
    twelve hundred lives.
    The waves of angry ocean clasped him
    merrily
    and kept in a secret place
    for all time to come.
If he would not have done so
the stream of time might have flown
in which direction
nobody would have known !
Lest might not be executed
the twelve hundred mansons.
The twelve year old boy in his later life
might have extreme excellence in craftsmanship
producing wonderful architecture,
amazing sculpture and iconography,
excelled more than that of the intricate artworks
of Sun temple including stone carving
of erotic senses.
    He might have turned down
    the pages of history.

After My Death

After my death
won't turn down the earth.
>The earth will continue
>to rotate daily around its own axis
>and revolve around the sun
>year after year.
>Seasons will change
>one after another,
>rain after summer
>spring after winter,
>all will happen as usual.

After my death,
as on today, the sun
will rise in the east
and set in the west;
in the darkness of night
will twinkle galaxy of stars;
the moon will appear
at specific time and site of the sky
between new moon and full moon day
and *vice versa*.
>After my death
>my kinships will take my cadaver
>to Swargadwâra at Puri.

> In procession of tears
> will perform my cremation rituals,
> bathing in the sea
> taking Mahaprasad of Lord Jagannath
> will return back taking my
> remains of the bone
> to solemnize further rituals.

Time will slip gradually
through the petals and thorns of the roses.
My kinships, as usual, will watch
the TV serials, sitting in the Ionox
will taste the popcorn of obliviousness,
to relax their minds will fly
to the romantic beach of Thailand
or to tulip gardens of the Netherlands.

> After my death
> won't turn down the earth.

Immersion of My Bone

For some days
will shed warm tears
my own kinships
after my demise
from this mortal earth,
but strange, people think it immortal,
wanna live for centuries.
      Then my kinships will devour
      cottage cheese fritters,
      tandoori chicken and what not,
      just as usual.
      Attend office, sign false bills
      play in the golf course,
      sitting in the air-conditioned halls
      will listen to music,
      may travel to foreign land
      in chattered aeroplane
      will be overhelmed with joy
      visualizing the natural beauties
      of Italy and France.
After my demise
my kinships and relatives
may forget the date and day
of my death anniversary.

The desire to lit an earthen lamp
might have gone out.
Anxiouslessly my heirs
may offer *Pinda*[1]
near the shore of *Bindu Sagar*[2]
or on the twenty-two steps
of Jagannath temple,
till immersion of my bone
in the roaring ocean
or in the polluted water
of the sacred Ganges.

■

---

[1] *Pinda:* Cooked rice-balls mixed with ghee and black sesame seeds offered to ancestors during Hindu funeral rites and ancestor worship.

[2] *Bindu Sagar:* is a lake in Bhubaneswar. According to legends, it was created by Lord Shiva by bringing water from all the holy places to quench the thirst of Goddess Parvati.

Invitation of Death

What's death?
When and why does it come?
 Will death whisper you:
 I'll come in certain year
 in certain month, in certain date and day
 and will knock thy door
 you must be ready !
Crawling and crawling you'll open the door
oozing out from you knee
drops of blood,
may be removed from your elbow
a piece of skin
in the rough stony road of time,
even if you supply caloric energy
willn't bend your fingers,
or else sleeping in the bed in disease
you'll yell: Open the door,
may be in a romantic dream
you would be flying in the sky
with an angel and by the
knocking sound in the door
may fall on the ground
and yell: Who is that rascal
disturbing me while visualizing

a delightful dream!
May be you'll open the door
even if suffering from deadly pain
lest a messenger of God may arrive,
closing the eyes if he touches you,
strange, you may become a healthy youngman !
But alas !
all your desires, aspirations
longings and passions
will be churned
when you'll hear that
the *Yamraj** has come
to take you with him
on the back of a buffaloo !

---

* *Yamaraj*: The God of death.

Epitaph

Once death had come
to my father
in the morning of ninth
new moon day of a winter.
    Honouring the death,
    we had taken him
    to *Swargadwâra* at Puri
    where after cremation
    all thought, his noble soul
    might have taken rest in heaven.
    Tears of my kinships
    mingled in the sea water of grief.
Around seven decades ago
death also came and took away
Mirâ nani, my elder sister
who was suffering from
an unknown fever
and had spent only
three springs in this world.
Narrated me all my relatives
how in grief my mother
again and again was crying aloud
and getting fainted on the bare ground.
    Calm and quietly death also

arrived one late night
a decade ago, and took away my ailing
mother
from the intensive care unit
of a corporate hospital in Bhubaneswar.
All we were stunted and dumbfounded,
took her cadaver
to the *Swargadwâra*.
Few days ago,
death came in disguise
as the quicksand of a river
took an engineering son of my friend
whirling deep into the river,
couldn't get his dead body
though all searched the entire river.
When will death come,
how will it come,
why will it come,
in which image will it come,
at which age of a person
will it come,
nobody has yet given
the correct answer.

PUBLISHED BOOKS OF THIS AUTHOR
I. LITERARY BOOKS
Odia Poetry Collections
1. 'Shâdhee', Unique Publishers, Cuttack, 2002.
2. 'Andhârare Indradhanu', Anwesana Prakashani, Bhubaneswar, 2007.
3. 'Nasta Nakhyatra', Sudhanya Prakashani, Bhubaneswar, 2013.
4. 'Sabdamananku Nei Swapna', Kahani, Cuttack, 2014.
5. 'Adrushya Chitrapata', Anwesana Prakashani, Bhubaneswar, 2015.
6. 'Panjurira Prajâpati', Publishing House, Bhubaneswar, 2017.
7. 'Nishabda Banshiswana', Black Eagle Books, USA, First International Edition, 2021.

English Poetry Transcreations
8. 'The Rainbow in Darkness', SSDN Publishers and Distributors, New Delhi, 2014.
9. 'The Butterfly of the Cage', Black Eagle Books, USA, First International Edition, 2023.

Short Story Collection
10. 'Marichikâre Manishatia', New Age, Balasore, 2000.

Popular Science Collections
11. 'Upakari Udvida' Dibyaduta Prakashani, Cuttack, 2003.
12. 'Udvidamânanka Madhyare Ghrunâ O Prema', Jagannath Rath, Cuttack, 2012.
13. 'Jin Bigyânara Jayajatrâ', Gyanajuga Publication, Bhubaneswar, 2014 (recipient of Odisha Bigyana Academy Award, 2015, Rajadhani Book Fair Award, 2014, and Kalinga Book Fair Award, 2016).
14. 'Mânaba Sebâre Udvida', Gyana Bigyanika, Cuttack, 2015 (Bhubaneswar Book Fair Award, 2017).
15. 'Bigyânara Darpanare Aji', Shakti Publishers, Cuttack,

2016.

16. 'Phala Khaibâ Sustha Rahibâ', Gyanajuga Publication, Bhubaneswar, 2023.

Scientific Novel

17. 'Mangala Pathe', Kitab Bhawan, Bhubaneswar, 2019

General Knowledge

18. 'Ajira Dibasa', Shakti Publishers, Cuttack, 2016

Editing Poetry Anthology

19. 'Jibana Marana Sakhâ', by Late Harihar Sahu, Gyanajuga Publication, Bhubaneswar, 2014.

II. SCIENCE TEXTBOOKS

Apart from the above literary books, Prof. Sahu has 33 science textbooks for secondary, higher secondary (CBSE/NCERT) and degree (CBCS) classes at state and national level. These science textbooks at degree level mainly include biological sciences like Plant Physiology, Plant Metabolism, Plant Biotechnology, Plant Ecology and Phytogeography, Biomolecule and Cell Biology, Molecular Biology (both for Botany and Zoology Honours), Genetics, Plant Breeding, Natural Resource Management, Microbial Physiology and Biochemistry etc.

Thus, he has in total 52 books to his credit uptill now.

BLACK EAGLE BOOKS

www.blackeaglebooks.org
info@blackeaglebooks.org

Black Eagle Books, an independent publisher, was founded as a nonprofit organization in April, 2019. It is our mission to connect and engage the Indian diaspora and the world at large with the best of works of world literature published on a collaborative platform, with special emphasis on foregrounding Contemporary Classics and New Writing.

www.ingramcontent.com/pod-product-compliance
Lightning Source LLC
Chambersburg PA
CBHW020539080526
44583CB00013B/908